The Magic of Me

New Beginnings

Look within to discover
your magic . . . .

Janie Emerson

ISBN: 978-0-9716320-4-2
Book design by Janie Emerson
Printed in the United States of America.

JEM Enterprises
La Jolla, California

ShamrockWisdom.com

DEDICATED TO

All who love magic.

All who know magic is
the positive power within us.

We are born with this power.
Embrace your magic
and share it....

INTRODUCTION

How to release your Magic

The Magic of Me contains joyful refections on life to guide you through each day. Use this magical book well. Select a new page and let its positive energy open your special magic.

Caress and handle this book often to make it truly powerful. Use it for affirmations in the morning to guide your day. Use it as an appreciation at night to begin your dreams.

The left side of each page has been left blank. Use it! Feel free to write your thoughts, draw your dreams, and open your magic.

Enjoy this special book. Make it yours. It is sent to you with love - to reflect your "Magic" to all in your life -

The true Magic of you.

Look within
to
discover
your Magic . . . .

I
look within
&
see
MAGIC –

Your
magic
is
everywhere . . . .

Spread
your wings
&
take
your space !

Be
positive
&
believe -

I want
to
be free
to
be me -

Believe -
it is
the key
to
it all -

Be
yourself
totally
&
happily
always -

Time'
to
love
myself -

Hugs
are important –

Hugs
heal . . . .

Celebrate
the
sheer joy
of
life –

I
make
fun miracles
&
happy
joy . . . .

Give

Love

&

Get

Joy -

Joy
is
my security
blanket -

The
magic is
within
me
always –

You
can trust
yourself,
too -

Time
for me to
be
my best
friend . . . .

All
is well –

Worry
not . . . .

I
honor what
works
for me . . . .

Trust

&

Believe . . . .

You
have "the
gift."

Share it !

I
see myself
&
love
"my me" . . . .

You
know life -
Laugh
&
enjoy
it all !

Laugh
with
Love -

Hold
tight to your
faith –
when needed . . . .

48

You
always
have
a
choice . . . .

I am
not
Everybody . . .
and
it is ok!

Follow
your instincts –
Even
the little
ones . . . .

Always –
Trust yourself
first !

We only
"get it"
by
doing "it"
ourselves –

Believe
and
you create
it so . . . .

I
believe in
my
dreams
always -

Give
thanks for
your
gift of
freedom -

I am
free
to express,
to create,
&
to be me -

Today
I appreciate
me -
just me

Give
the gift
of
wings
to fly –

Soar
with the joy
of
each day . . . .

Allow
the fun -
It is
life . . . .

Be
your best . . . .
Then
believe
it
every day –

Always
focus on
your
reality . . . .

Feel
the
limitless
joy -

Relax
&
let life
flow -

Happiness
is
feeling the
joyful
bubbles
inside . . . .

Love
it all
&
create
your magic . . . .

Stretch
for
your
dreams -

Be

&

Believe

I
choose to
live
&
enjoy
my life
completely -

Adventure
is
life's
spice . . . .

Today
I
celebrate
all
of me -

Enjoy the
moment -
It is
all you
have . . . .

I
take my
power
&
know it
is me -

Joy
is who
we
are -

ABOUT THE AUTHOR

JANIE EMERSON

Janie Emerson is the author of the successful *Appreciate Each Day, Guided By Animal Angels*, and *Walking With Angels*. Her writings appear in newspapers and magazines. She has won national awards for her poetry and is a respected consultant and acclaimed speaker.

The inspiration for her writings comes from life. Janie's work gives balance, insight and focus to life's events. Her intent is to empower and to enhance your life.

Janie lives in La Jolla, CA with her husband Bob and her beloved Westies. She has been an advocate for women owned businesses nationally and an active community leader. Janie is currently working on two great new projects.